FORTNITE: ULTIMATE STRATEGIES AND SECRETS

TRAVIS HEMBREE

ISBN:

DEDICATION

This book is dedicated to all Fortnite players who strive to improve, connect, and create every day on the island. May these pages inspire you to reach new heights and explore every aspect of Fortnite with confidence and creativity.

CONTENTS

Table of Contents

1. Introduction to Fortnite

2. Mastering the Basics

3. Essential Building Techniques

4. Competitive Strategy and Training

5. Exploring Fortnite Lore and Storylines

6. The Cultural Impact of Fortnite

7. Training to Become a Pro Player

8. Game Updates and the Ever-Evolving Meta

9. The Future of Fortnite

10. The Lasting Legacy of Fortnite

11. Player Resources and Interactive Tools

12. Thank You and Final Thoughts

ACKNOWLEDGMENTS

Creating Fortnite Ultimate Strategies and Secrets was a team effort, and I'd like to extend my deepest gratitude to everyone who made it possible. Thank you to my family and friends for their encouragement and support throughout this project. To the Fortnite community, your passion and dedication are the driving force behind this book, and I am constantly inspired by your skill, creativity, and spirit. Special thanks to Epic Games for crafting such an incredible world that continues to bring people together and foster unforgettable experiences.

CHAPTER 1: INTRODUCTION TO FORTNITE

1.1 Understanding the Fortnite Phenomenon

The Origins of Fortnite

Fortnite was originally developed as a player-versus-environment (PvE) game mode called *Save the World*, where players would build defenses to survive waves of enemies. But in September 2017, Epic Games introduced the *Battle Royale* mode, inspired by games like *PUBG* and the last-player-standing format. This shift transformed Fortnite into a global sensation almost overnight, offering a free-to-play game with unique building mechanics that set it apart from other battle royale titles.

Why Fortnite Became a Phenomenon

Fortnite's success can be attributed to several key factors:

- **Accessible Gameplay**: Unlike many other battle royale games, Fortnite is free-to-play on all major platforms, from consoles to mobile devices, making it accessible to a wide audience.
- **Constant Updates**: Fortnite's commitment to frequent updates and seasonal content keeps gameplay fresh and exciting. Each season introduces new skins, events, mechanics, and map changes, ensuring players always have something to look forward to.
- **Cultural Crossovers**: From *Marvel* heroes to *Star Wars*

characters, Fortnite's pop culture crossovers bring players closer to their favorite franchises. Virtual concerts featuring artists like Travis Scott and Ariana Grande turned Fortnite into a digital social space, bringing music and gaming together in ways never seen before.

1.2 Battle Royale and Game Mode Overview

Battle Royale Overview

In *Battle Royale*, 100 players are dropped onto an island and compete to be the last one standing. Players start with no weapons or items, relying on quick decision-making, looting, and building to survive.

Flow of a Typical Match

Understanding the flow of a Fortnite match is crucial for new players. Here's a breakdown:

1. **Drop Zone**: Choosing where to land can define your early-game experience. High-traffic areas offer great loot but come with higher risks, while remote areas are safer but may lack resources.
2. **Early Looting and Combat**: Collect resources and weapons to build your loadout. Watch out for nearby players, and stay alert for quick early fights.
3. **Mid-game Survival**: With fewer players remaining, focus on moving with the storm circle while gathering materials and watching for opponents.
4. **Final Circle**: The endgame takes place in a small, shrinking safe zone, where players rely on strategic building, combat skills, and timing to secure the Victory Royale.

Different Game Modes

- **Solo, Duos, Squads**: Each mode demands a unique approach:
  - *Solo*: You're on your own, so strategy and

situational awareness are essential.

- *Duos and Squads*: Teamwork and communication become critical, as you rely on your teammates for support and revival.
- **Creative Mode**: A sandbox environment where you can build custom maps and games, perfect for honing skills, practicing builds, or just having fun with friends.
- **Limited-Time Modes (LTMs)**: Fortnite periodically introduces LTMs with unique rules, offering a fresh experience and allowing players to test different playstyles. Examples include *Sniper Shootout* and *50v50*.

1.3 Basic Controls and Settings

Control Customization

Whether you're playing on PC, console, or mobile, customizing your controls can enhance your gameplay. For example, on PC, many pro players map building keys close to their movement keys for quick access. On consoles, remapping the jump button to the left or right stick allows for faster aiming and building.

Settings for Optimal Performance

- **Graphics Settings**: Reducing settings like shadows and post-processing can improve FPS, especially on older PCs and consoles.
- **Recommended Keybinds**: Optimal keybinds can improve response times, especially in building. Include a suggested setup for both PC and console players, focusing on simplicity and speed.

Accessibility Settings

For players with auditory or visual impairments, Fortnite offers settings like *Visualize Sound Effects*, which displays audio cues on-screen. This feature is also useful for all players to detect distant enemies and loot.

1.4 The Building vs. Combat Dynamic

Why Building Changes the Game

Unlike other battle royales, Fortnite's building mechanic enables players to create structures on the fly, adding a layer of strategy that affects every engagement. Building provides protection, allows for positioning advantages, and can be used offensively to pressure opponents.

Learning to Build Under Pressure

To become proficient in building, start with Creative Mode. Practicing basic structures—such as walls for cover or ramps for high ground—can make a difference in your survival rate.

- **Quick Builds to Practice**: Start with the "ramp wall" combo, which creates a simple structure to protect yourself while advancing toward an opponent. Practice building and editing in a safe environment until it becomes second nature.

Defensive vs. Offensive Building

- **Defensive**: Use walls and ramps to shield yourself from enemy fire. Building "boxes" (1x1 structures) is effective for healing or reloading.
- **Offensive**: High ground is often the key to winning a fight. Building up allows you to shoot down at opponents, making it harder for them to hit you while giving you clear sightlines.

1.5 Looting and Survival Essentials

Loot Tiers and Rarities

Fortnite's loot system is color-coded by rarity, affecting a weapon's damage and effectiveness. Here's a quick guide:

- **Gray**: Common
- **Green**: Uncommon
- **Blue**: Rare
- **Purple**: Epic

- **Gold**: Legendary
- **Exotic**: Unique items available in limited locations.

Starting Strong – Choosing a Drop Zone

Choosing a landing spot can make or break your match. High-traffic areas like *Tilted Towers* and *Lazy Lake* have abundant loot but high competition, while quieter areas like *Misty Meadows* offer safer starts with moderate loot. Consider the flight path of the Battle Bus, and choose a spot that aligns with your strategy.

Survival Tips

- **Resource Gathering**: Use your pickaxe to gather materials (wood, stone, metal) early on. These are essential for building, which you'll need both offensively and defensively.
- **Storm Awareness**: The storm gradually shrinks, forcing players into a smaller safe zone. Keep an eye on your minimap to avoid getting caught outside the circle, as the storm will damage you over time.

1.6 Introduction to Fortnite's Social and Interactive Features

Social Features

Fortnite's social aspect lets you squad up with friends, join parties, and use in-game voice chat. *Emotes* add a playful element, allowing players to communicate or celebrate in non-verbal ways. In competitive play, respecting the social norms of the game, like avoiding intentional teaming in solo modes, maintains a fair environment.

Community and Events

Fortnite regularly hosts in-game events, from holiday celebrations to virtual concerts, making it more than just a game but a social platform where players can connect and celebrate shared interests.

- **Recent Event Example**: Highlight a recent live event, explaining how Fortnite has integrated pop culture in real-time, creating experiences that go beyond standard gameplay.

CHAPTER 2: MASTERING GAMEPLAY

2.1 Building Fundamentals and Advanced Techniques

The Importance of Building

Building is a critical skill in Fortnite, providing a unique layer of gameplay that can protect, position, and confuse opponents. In this section, we'll go beyond the basics to help players understand when and how to build effectively.

Basic Structures for Survival

- **Walls and Ramps**: Walls protect you from incoming fire, while ramps give you height, an essential advantage in Fortnite. Practice building walls and ramps quickly to shield yourself during ambushes or to gain elevation.
- **Boxing Up**: Building a 1x1 box (a small structure with walls, a floor, and a roof) is an effective tactic for healing, reloading, or repositioning in combat.

Advanced Building Techniques

- **Ramp-Rush Technique**: The ramp-rush involves building ramps toward an enemy to close the distance while gaining height. For added protection, place walls in front of the ramps as you advance.
- **90s**: A "90" is a rapid technique used to gain vertical

height by turning and placing walls and ramps in quick succession. Practicing 90s helps you take the high ground efficiently, especially useful in build fights.

- **Tunneling**: In the late-game when the circle is small, tunneling lets you move while staying protected. Practice creating tunnels (building a small enclosed space with walls, floors, and roofs) to advance safely toward the safe zone.
- **Box Fighting**: Box fighting is an essential skill in close-range combat. By trapping yourself and your opponent in a 1x1 box, you can control edits and catch your enemy off guard. Learn to edit quickly and effectively, creating windows and doors to shoot from and reset for defense.

Editing Practice

Editing structures allows you to modify your builds in real time, creating windows, doors, or half-walls for strategic peeks and attacks.

- **Essential Edits**: Practice creating windows for quick shots, corner edits for surprise attacks, and ramp flips to disorient opponents.
- **Drills**: Use Creative Mode to practice specific edits repeatedly until they become muscle memory. This will improve your speed and accuracy in live games.

2.2 Weapon Types and Combat Basics

Weapon Types and Rarities

Fortnite's variety of weapons requires players to understand the strengths and weaknesses of each type. Here's a quick breakdown:

- **Assault Rifles**: Versatile for mid-range combat. Variants include burst-fire and scoped assault rifles, useful for precise shots.
- **Shotguns**: Powerful for close-quarters combat. Choose between Pump (high damage, slow fire rate) and

Tactical (lower damage, faster rate).

- **SMGs**: Ideal for rapid-fire, close-range encounters. Excellent for quick follow-ups after a shotgun shot.
- **Sniper Rifles**: Best for long-range eliminations. The bolt-action sniper deals significant damage but requires accuracy.
- **Explosives**: Grenades, Rocket Launchers, and C4 offer area damage, especially effective against enemy structures.

Effective Loadouts

A balanced loadout includes:

- **Close-Range**: Shotgun or SMG for high DPS in close encounters.
- **Mid-Range**: Assault Rifle or Tactical Shotgun for versatile situations.
- **Long-Range**: Sniper or scoped assault rifle if you prefer distance engagements.
- **Healing Items**: Always carry healing items or shields to recover after fights.

Combat Tips for Beginners

- **Peek Shooting**: Use structures or natural cover to peek and shoot, then retreat to minimize exposure.
- **Movement**: Constant movement reduces your chances of being an easy target. Jump, strafe, and use cover.
- **Weapon Switching**: Instead of reloading in the middle of a fight, switch to a secondary weapon to maintain pressure.

2.3 Strategies for Surviving Early, Mid, and Late Game

Early Game: Landing and Initial Looting

- **Choose a Smart Drop Spot**: High-traffic areas offer better loot but more immediate combat; quieter areas give time to gather resources without high risk.
- **Looting Efficiency**: Quickly gather resources, shields,

and weapons. Prioritize shields and a weapon before exploring further.

- **Resource Gathering**: Start gathering materials early on, as they're essential for building and defending in future engagements.

Mid-Game: Rotations and Positioning

- **Moving with the Storm**: As the storm circle shrinks, plan your route to stay within the safe zone while avoiding unnecessary fights.
- **Choosing Engagements**: Avoid engaging in every fight. Third-party engagements (joining an ongoing fight) are often advantageous, as both enemies may be distracted or weakened.
- **Resource Management**: Continue gathering materials, especially wood, which is useful for quick builds. Reserve harder materials like stone and metal for late-game builds.

Late Game: Surviving in the Final Circle

- **Controlled Building**: Conserve materials by building only when necessary. Overbuilding can waste resources crucial for the final showdown.
- **Positioning for Advantage**: Secure high ground or stay near the edge of the storm circle, where you can see approaching players and avoid being sandwiched.
- **Stay Calm**: In high-stakes final circles, stay focused. Take controlled actions and wait for opponents to make mistakes, capitalizing on opportunities rather than rushing.

2.4 High Ground and Terrain Advantage

Why High Ground Matters

High ground gives players a clear line of sight and forces opponents to look up, which slows their response time and accuracy. Building ramps or reaching natural high points can make the difference between winning and losing a fight.

Building to Secure High Ground

- **Ramp and Wall Combinations**: Combine ramps and walls to build upward while staying protected.
- **Protected High Ground Retakes**: When opponents are above you, use walls and ramps to climb back up without exposing yourself.
- **Avoid Overbuilding**: Reaching the high ground is important, but wasting materials can leave you vulnerable in the late game. Use only as many builds as necessary.

2.5 Inventory Management and Loadout Strategy

Healing and Shields

Keep at least one healing item (such as Medkits or Bandages) and one shield item. Big Shield Potions offer the most protection, but Minis (Small Shield Potions) are quicker to use. Slurp items are valuable because they restore both health and shields over time.

Utility Items

Items like grenades, shockwave grenades, and launch pads offer strategic advantages. Use them to reposition, escape difficult fights, or surprise opponents.

Optimizing Your Loadout

- **Two Weapon Limit**: Stick to two primary weapons (such as an Assault Rifle and Shotgun) to make room for shields, healing items, and utility.
- **Adapt to the Situation**: Swap items based on the current phase of the game. For example, in the late game, prioritize shields over healing items to survive intense fights.

2.6 Practice Tips and Creative Mode Drills

Building Drills

- **Speed Building**: Practice building walls and ramps in quick succession to gain confidence and muscle memory.
- **90s Drill**: Work on perfecting the "90s" technique for high ground advantage. Set a timer and see how quickly you can build 90s consistently.
- **Box Fight Scenarios**: Practice box fighting with a friend or in Creative Mode. Focus on editing, peeking, and resetting builds for quick offensive plays.

Aim and Accuracy Drills

- **Target Practice Maps**: Fortnite Creative has dedicated maps designed to improve your aim. Practice hitting moving targets to increase your accuracy in combat.
- **Tracking and Flick Shots**: Use aim trainers or target practice maps to work on tracking moving targets and making quick flick shots, both essential for combat.

Regular Gameplay Practice

- **Arena Mode**: Test your skills in Fortnite's ranked mode, Arena, to practice against competitive players. You'll learn to manage pressure and adapt to more challenging opponents.
- **Custom Matches**: Playing custom matches with friends can simulate a competitive environment and help refine your building, aiming, and game sense.

CHAPTER 3: MASTERING ADVANCED STRATEGIES

3.1 Building Like a Pro: Advanced Techniques

Mastering 90s for Height Control

The "90s" technique is essential for quickly gaining vertical height over opponents. Here's how to perfect it:

- **The Technique**: Build walls and ramps in a spiral while jumping and turning 90 degrees. This creates a tower that's difficult for opponents to shoot down.
- **Practice Tip**: Start slow in Creative Mode, focusing on accurate placement. Gradually increase speed as you build muscle memory.

Ramp-Rush Variations

- **Standard Ramp-Rush**: Place a ramp toward your opponent while advancing. Add walls in front to shield from enemy fire.
- **Double-Ramp and Wall**: Build two ramps side-by-side with walls below, providing double protection.
- **Side-Ramp**: Use side ramps to approach enemies from

an angle, allowing you to gain height without exposing yourself directly.

Piece Control

Piece control involves claiming and editing structures around your opponent to limit their movement and gain an advantage. Practice controlling structures in close quarters to create openings for attacks.

- **The Trap and Edit Combo**: Box your opponent in, then edit walls or ramps to catch them off guard.
- **Practice Drill**: In Creative Mode, practice boxing up a moving target (like a friend or bot), trapping them within a structure to limit their options.

Tunneling Techniques

Tunneling is crucial in the late game when circles are small, and you need safe movement. Here are some tunnel variations:

- **Single Tunnel**: Place a floor, walls, and a roof in quick succession as you move forward.
- **Double Tunnel**: Create parallel tunnels to protect against enemies on both sides.
- **Diagonal Tunnel**: For crossing open areas under fire, move diagonally while building walls, floors, and roofs.

3.2 Editing Mastery for Combat Advantage

Why Editing is Key in Advanced Combat

Editing allows you to surprise your opponent with quick shots while remaining shielded. Good editing skills can make or break close-quarters encounters.

Essential Edits

- **Window Edit**: Create a small window to peek and shoot. Use this for safe, controlled engagements.
- **Top Corner Edit**: Edit the top two squares of a wall to create a gap you can shoot through.
- **Ramp Flips**: When you're on a ramp, edit it to change

direction quickly, confusing your opponent.

Editing Drills in Creative Mode

- **Edit Course Practice**: Use Creative Mode's edit courses to practice speed and accuracy. Start with simple edits, then progress to complex combinations.
- **Quick Reset Practice**: In close-range combat, edit walls quickly for offensive shots, then reset them immediately to protect yourself from counterattacks.

3.3 Advanced Combat Strategies

Aiming Techniques for Competitive Play

- **Flick Shots**: Learn to make quick, precise shots by practicing flicks in Creative Mode or with aim trainers.
- **Tracking**: Tracking is essential for sustained fire. Practice staying on target with moving enemies by focusing on smooth, controlled movements.

Strategic Reloading and Weapon Switching

- **Weapon Cycling**: In close fights, switch weapons instead of reloading to maintain pressure on your opponent.
- **Reload Timing**: Use breaks in combat (like building for cover) to reload safely and stay prepared for the next encounter.

Cover and Peek Shooting

- **Right-Hand Peek Advantage**: Fortnite's camera angle gives players an advantage when peeking from the right. Position yourself accordingly to reduce exposure.
- **Corner Peeking**: Use edited walls to peek around corners safely, giving you visibility while protecting most of your body.

Close-Range Box Fighting

- **Boxing Your Opponent**: Build a box around your opponent and control the space to dictate their movement.
- **Edit and Replace Tactic**: Replace your opponent's walls with yours, allowing you to edit for a shot and reset to defend.

3.4 Effective Use of Loadouts and Utility Items

Choosing the Right Loadout for Each Situation

- **Close Combat Loadout**: Focus on shotguns and SMGs, along with healing items for quick recovery.
- **Balanced Loadout**: A versatile setup with an assault rifle, shotgun, and healing items.
- **Long-Range Loadout**: Carry a sniper or scoped weapon for distant engagements, plus mobility items like shockwave grenades or launch pads.

Utility Item Strategy

- **Grenades and Explosives**: Use these to apply pressure, break down structures, or flush opponents out of cover.
- **Launch Pads and Shockwave Grenades**: Great for quick escapes, surprise attacks, or fast rotations. Carry these especially in the endgame for quick repositioning.

3.5 High Ground Retakes

Why High Ground is Crucial

The high ground provides a tactical advantage, as you have better visibility and control over the battlefield. When the high ground is lost, these retake strategies can help you regain it.

High Ground Retake Techniques

- **Protected Side Ramp Retake**: Build ramps to the side of your opponent's position, adding walls for protection.

This allows you to reach high ground without directly exposing yourself.

- **Cone and Floor Placement**: When moving upward, place cones and floors on top of the enemy's builds to prevent them from following you or blocking you.
- **Jumping to the Side**: Sometimes a side jump can be enough to throw off your opponent and reclaim the high ground.

Practice for Consistency

- **Creative Mode Drills**: Practice high ground retakes in Creative Mode by setting up scenarios where you start below a ramp or platform and work on reclaiming high ground against an imaginary opponent.
- **High Ground vs. Low Ground Combat**: In real matches, practice controlling high ground with efficient building and positioning rather than unnecessary building, conserving materials for the final circle.

3.6 Timing and Rotations in the Late Game

Understanding Rotations

As the safe zone shrinks, rotating effectively (moving strategically within the storm circle) becomes essential to survival in the endgame.

Rotation Strategies

- **Early Rotation**: Moving early gives you time to establish a secure position and build a defensive structure.
- **Late Rotation**: If you're confident in your building skills, rotating late can allow you to catch opponents unaware as they move into the zone.

Using Mobility Items

- **Launch Pads**: Use launch pads to cover large distances quickly or to escape dangerous situations.

- **Shockwave Grenades**: These can propel you over enemy structures or into the safe zone at the last second.
- **Vehicles**: Cars and boats can be useful but may attract attention. Use them strategically to cover distance quickly.

Managing Resources and Health

- **Material Conservation**: Avoid overbuilding in the mid-game so you have enough materials for the endgame. Stone and metal are ideal for final circles as they offer more durability.
- **Health and Shield Management**: Try to enter the final circles with full health and shields. If you're low, prioritize healing safely before moving.

3.7 Mind Games and Psychological Tactics

Baiting and Faking

- **Sound Baiting**: Use sounds to mislead opponents. For example, fake a healing sound to lure in aggressive players and then ambush them.
- **Building Fake Structures**: Build ramps or walls in a way that suggests you're advancing in a particular direction, then change paths to surprise your opponent.

Mental Preparation

- **Staying Calm in High-Stakes Situations**: The final circle is intense. Take a breath, focus, and stay in control. Panicking can lead to mistakes.
- **Reading Opponents**: Observe your opponent's building and movement patterns. Experienced players can often predict enemy behavior, giving them a split-second advantage.

Outsmarting Opponents with Quick Edits

- **Edit Delays**: Occasionally fake an edit to bait your opponent into exposing themselves, then complete the edit for a surprise attack.
- **Cornering**: Trap opponents in corners or limited spaces where they can't escape, forcing them into predictable patterns.

CHAPTER 4: THE COMPETITIVE SCENE OF FORTNITE

4.1 Overview of Competitive Fortnite

The Rise of Competitive Fortnite

Since Fortnite's release, it has rapidly become a major force in esports. Epic Games has organized large-scale tournaments, such as the Fortnite World Cup, attracting millions of viewers and providing a platform for talented players worldwide. Fortnite's unique combination of building and combat, combined with a massive player base, has helped it establish a dynamic and competitive scene.

Tournament Formats

- **Solo, Duo, and Trio Tournaments**: Each mode offers different challenges. Solo tournaments test individual skills, while Duos and Trios add a layer of teamwork and strategy.
- **FNCS (Fortnite Champion Series)**: The FNCS is Fortnite's premier tournament series, featuring multiple qualifying rounds and culminating in regional finals.
- **Cash Cups**: Weekly tournaments where players

compete for cash prizes, open to players at all skill levels. Cash Cups provide great practice and a taste of competitive play.

- **Arena Mode**: Fortnite's ranked mode where players earn points to advance through divisions, facing increasingly difficult opponents as they progress.

Competitive Seasons and Meta Changes

Each season brings new weapons, mechanics, and strategies, shaping the competitive "meta" (the most effective ways to play based on current features). Staying updated on changes and adapting quickly is crucial to staying competitive.

4.2 Training and Practicing for Competitive Play

Building a Practice Routine

Consistency is key in competitive play. Here's how to structure a practice routine:

- **Creative Mode Drills**: Dedicate time to building, editing, and aiming exercises in Creative Mode. Use specific maps designed for practicing 90s, box fighting, and tunneling.
- **VOD Review**: Watch replays of your matches to analyze mistakes, successful strategies, and decision-making processes. This self-assessment helps identify areas for improvement.
- **Arena Mode for Scrimmage Practice**: Use Arena Mode to play against skilled opponents, simulating a competitive environment. Practice rotations, resource management, and endgame strategies.

Collaborative Training with Teammates

For Duo and Trio tournaments, effective teamwork is essential. Spend time practicing with your teammates:

- **Communication Drills**: Practice concise callouts for enemy positions, rotations, and resource sharing.
- **Role Definition**: In Trio play, assign specific roles (e.g.,

one player focuses on building, another on scouting, and the third on supporting or healing).

- **Endgame Practice**: Use Creative Mode or custom lobbies to simulate endgame scenarios, focusing on rotations, positioning, and material management.

4.3 Competitive Strategies for Each Game Stage

Early Game Strategy

- **Landing Strategy**: Choose a drop spot with reliable loot and minimal player traffic. This allows for a safer start to gather resources without immediate combat.
- **Efficient Looting**: Prioritize gathering shields, materials, and weapons quickly to be prepared for unexpected encounters.
- **Establishing Control**: Dominate your drop location by engaging and eliminating nearby players to secure the area for additional looting.

Mid-Game Strategy

- **Rotations and Positioning**: Plan rotations to stay within the storm circle while avoiding high-traffic areas. Take advantage of natural cover and structures along the way.
- **Choosing Engagements Wisely**: Avoid unnecessary fights that could drain resources or reveal your position. Instead, look for opportunities to third-party fights for easier eliminations.
- **Material and Ammo Management**: Ensure you have ample resources for endgame. Continue gathering materials, focusing on stone and metal, which are more durable.

Endgame Strategy

- **Safe Zone Awareness**: Position yourself near the edge of the safe zone to reduce exposure to enemies and gain better visibility.

- **Controlled Building**: Use materials efficiently, building only when necessary. Conserve resources for high-pressure moments in the final circles.
- **Staying Calm Under Pressure**: Focus on situational awareness and clear thinking. Don't panic if you're low on resources or health; wait for an opponent to make a mistake you can exploit.

4.4 Mental Preparation and Focus

Building Mental Resilience

The mental demands of competitive play are high. Develop habits to manage pressure effectively:

- **Staying Positive and Focused**: Maintaining a positive outlook, even after losses, helps you stay motivated. Focus on learning from each match rather than dwelling on mistakes.
- **Mindfulness Techniques**: Use breathing exercises to stay calm, especially in the final circles. Practicing mindfulness can help you keep your cool in intense situations.
- **Goal Setting**: Set achievable, short-term goals (like reaching a new rank in Arena Mode) and long-term goals (like qualifying for FNCS) to stay focused.

Managing Fatigue

Competitive gaming can be physically and mentally exhausting. To prevent burnout:

- **Take Regular Breaks**: Short breaks between matches can help reset your focus.
- **Sleep and Hydration**: Good sleep and staying hydrated are essential for peak performance. Competitive play requires sharp reflexes and concentration, both of which are improved with proper rest and hydration.
- **Exercise for Focus**: Physical activity, even light exercise, can improve focus and reduce stress.

Incorporate a daily routine to support overall well-being.

4.5 Community and Networking

Joining Fortnite's Competitive Community

Networking within the Fortnite community can open doors for scrim practice, team-building, and even sponsorship opportunities. Here's how to get involved:

- **Discord Servers**: Join competitive Fortnite servers to meet players at various skill levels, find scrim lobbies, and share tips.
- **Twitter and Social Media**: Many competitive players use Twitter to connect, announce scrim lobbies, and share gameplay highlights. Follow top players and join conversations.
- **Reddit and Forums**: Reddit communities like r/FortniteCompetitive offer insights, discussions, and tips. Use these forums to stay informed and engage with other players.

Networking with Potential Teammates

Competitive Fortnite is highly team-oriented in Duos and Trios. Building a reliable team is essential:

- **Finding Teammates with Similar Goals**: Look for players who share your skill level and competitive ambitions. Use Discord or Twitter to find scrim partners.
- **Consistent Practice**: Developing a strong team dynamic takes time. Practice regularly with teammates to build communication and synergy.

Staying Professional Online

Maintaining a positive reputation in the competitive scene can attract more opportunities:

- **Respecting Opponents**: Even in the heat of competition, stay respectful toward opponents. Good sportsmanship reflects well on you and can help establish a positive reputation.

- **Avoiding Toxic Behavior**: Emotions run high in competitive gaming, but avoiding negative or toxic behavior contributes to a supportive community.

4.6 Content Creation and Building a Personal Brand

The Role of Content Creation

Creating and sharing Fortnite content can help build a personal brand, attract sponsors, and grow your following:

- **Streaming**: Platforms like Twitch and YouTube are popular for streaming Fortnite gameplay. Streaming regularly helps you connect with an audience and showcase your skills.
- **Gameplay Highlights**: Share clips of impressive eliminations, creative building, or clutch wins on social media to attract attention.
- **Educational Content**: Sharing tips and tutorials on specific skills (like building or aiming) can help grow your reputation as an expert and attract followers interested in learning.

Developing a Social Media Presence

Consistency and interaction are key for growing a following:

- **Regular Posting**: Share highlights, updates on your progress, and personal insights to keep your audience engaged.
- **Engagement with Fans**: Respond to comments, host Q&A sessions, and acknowledge your followers to build a loyal community.

Finding Sponsorships and Partnerships

Once you have a growing following, sponsorships can provide financial support and opportunities:

- **Brand Partnerships**: Reach out to brands aligned with your values and audience, such as gaming gear companies.

- **Social Media Reach**: Many sponsors are interested in players with strong social media presence. Focus on building engagement (likes, shares, and comments) as well as follower count.

4.7 The Future of Competitive Fortnite

The Evolution of Fortnite Esports

Epic Games continues to invest in Fortnite's esports scene, adding new features and increasing prize pools:

- **New Tournament Formats**: As Fortnite continues to grow, expect to see unique formats and modes (such as Solo Cash Cups or one-off LTMs) added to the competitive mix.
- **Cross-Platform Competitive Play**: Epic Games may expand cross-platform play to include more competitive modes, allowing players from different platforms to compete on a level playing field.
- **Global Events and Sponsorships**: Fortnite's global appeal could lead to even larger international tournaments and brand sponsorships in the future.

Preparing for What's Next

Stay ahead of the competition by staying informed:

- **Following Updates and Patches**: Regularly check patch notes for updates on weapon balance, map changes, and mechanics that affect the competitive meta.
- **Adapting to Meta Shifts**: As new weapons or items are introduced, adapt your strategies and loadouts to stay competitive.

Building a Lasting Career in Fortnite

For those looking to make Fortnite a long-term career, balancing competitive play with content creation and networking is essential. The skills and connections you build can open doors beyond Fortnite, potentially leading to other gaming and content opportunities.

CHAPTER 5: FORTNITE LORE AND STORYLINES

5.1 The Origins of Fortnite's Story

The Zero Point: The Heart of Fortnite's Universe

At the center of Fortnite's lore is the *Zero Point*, a powerful energy source located beneath the island. It connects different realities, serving as the focal point of many conflicts. Control over the Zero Point is a major goal for different factions in the Fortnite universe, each with its own agenda.

The Island and Its Evolution

The Fortnite island is not a static battleground—it's an ever-changing environment influenced by the Zero Point. Over the seasons, the island has undergone dramatic transformations, from meteor impacts and floods to dimensional rifts and black holes. These changes often coincide with major in-game events, introducing new areas and gameplay mechanics.

The Loop: An Endless Battle

The Loop is a mysterious phenomenon that resets the island every 22 minutes, trapping its inhabitants in a continuous cycle of battle. Players, known as *Loopers*, are aware of the Loop, and some characters have tried to escape it. The Loop explains why each match resets and why players return to the island after being eliminated.

5.2 KEY FACTIONS AND CHARACTERS

The Seven

The Seven are a group of enigmatic warriors from different realities, dedicated to freeing the island and the Zero Point from external control. Each member has unique abilities and plays a significant role in the storyline.

- **The Visitor**: The first member introduced in Chapter 1, Season 4, The Visitor arrived on the island in a meteor and initiated the first major event by creating a rocket.
- **The Scientist and The Paradigm**: Additional members of The Seven, each with unique knowledge and technology. The Scientist specializes in building, while The Paradigm has extensive knowledge of the Zero Point.
- **The Foundation**: Voiced by Dwayne "The Rock" Johnson, The Foundation is the leader of The Seven and a central figure in the conflict against the Imagined Order (IO).

The Imagined Order (IO)

The IO is a shadowy organization that controls the island and manipulates the Loop for their own purposes. Their leader, Doctor Slone, is known for her calculated tactics and determination to control the Zero Point.

- **Doctor Slone**: A high-ranking IO agent who leads various operations to maintain control over the Loop and the Zero Point. She has clashed with The Seven multiple times.

- **IO Guards and Henchmen**: The organization employs guards and agents to protect their interests on the island and maintain control over key areas.

Other Important Characters

- **Jonesy**: A recurring character in Fortnite, Jonesy represents players in the Fortnite storyline. He worked for the IO but eventually joined forces with The Seven to free the island from the Loop.
- **Midas**: A central figure in Chapter 2, Midas is known for his "golden touch" and leads a faction called *The Agency*. His actions led to major events like *The Device* that temporarily broke the Loop.

5.3 MAJOR STORYLINE EVENTS AND ARCS

The Meteor Event (Chapter 1, Season 4)

A massive meteor crashed into the island, creating *Dusty Divot* and marking the arrival of The Visitor. This event introduced players to Fortnite's first major storyline and the existence of The Seven.

The Cube and Butterfly Events (Chapters 1 & 2)

Kevin the Cube, a mysterious purple cube, appeared on the island, rolling across the landscape and leaving runes. It eventually transformed Loot Lake into a bouncy surface and played a significant role in Chapter 2's storyline.

The End Event (Chapter 1 Finale)

In one of the most iconic events in gaming history, the island was consumed by a black hole, leading to the end of Chapter 1. This event left players in suspense for days before Chapter 2 began with a brand-new map and storyline.

The Galactus Event (Chapter 2, Season 4)

In a Marvel-themed season, the giant cosmic villain *Galactus* attempted to consume the Zero Point. Players joined forces with heroes like *Iron Man* and *Thor* to stop him, culminating in an epic battle that saved the island.

The Zero Crisis Finale (Chapter 2, Season 6)

This event focused on *Agent Jones* and *The Foundation* as they tried to stabilize the Zero Point. The event introduced players to The Foundation and set the stage for the ongoing conflict between The Seven and the IO.

The Collision Event (Chapter 3, Season 2)

In a climactic battle, The Seven fought against the IO, aided by a massive Mecha robot that came to the island's rescue. This event marked a turning point in the fight between The Seven and the IO, temporarily disrupting the IO's influence on the island.

5.4 CROSSOVERS AND ALTERNATE REALITIES

One of Fortnite's unique features is its crossovers with other universes. Through the Zero Point, characters from different realities—like *Marvel*, *Star Wars*, *DC Comics*, and *Street Fighter*—have entered Fortnite's world.

Marvel Crossovers

Fortnite has collaborated with Marvel on multiple occasions, bringing characters like *Spider-Man*, *Thanos*, and the *X-Men* to the island. These crossovers often tie into the storyline, with characters becoming part of the conflict over the Zero Point.

Star Wars Universe

Fortnite's Star Wars events introduced lightsabers, characters like *Darth Vader* and *The Mandalorian*, and themed areas on the island. These crossovers allowed players to wield iconic Star Wars weapons and interact with beloved characters.

DC and Other Franchises

Batman, *Superman*, *Harley Quinn*, and others have also joined the Fortnite universe. These crossovers sometimes feature unique story elements, such as Batman's investigation of the Zero Point, adding new lore to the Fortnite storyline.

Impact of Crossovers on Fortnite's Storyline

Each crossover is more than just a cosmetic addition. Fortnite's storyline integrates these characters, creating a true multiverse where characters from different realities interact, forming alliances and rivalries in the battle for the island.

5.5 THE EVOLUTION OF FORTNITE'S LORE THROUGH SEASONS

CHAPTER 1: THE FOUNDATION OF THE STORY

- **Key Themes**: The Visitor, Kevin the Cube, and the Rocket Launch. These events laid the groundwork for the existence of The Seven and the influence of the Zero Point.

CHAPTER 2: THE LOOP AND NEW CHARACTERS

- **Introduction of the Imagined Order**: With the addition of the IO, Fortnite's storyline deepened. The island transformed in response to new events like Midas's Device and the rise of Marvel heroes.
- **Seasonal Changes**: Each season introduced new map changes tied to the storyline, from flooding to introducing secret bases.

CHAPTER 3: EXPANDED CONFLICTS

- **Focus on The Seven vs. IO**: This chapter saw increased conflict between The Seven and the IO, including the Collision event and the arrival of new characters like The Foundation.
- **New Threats**: Additional villains and hazards, such as Dr. Slone's operations, kept players engaged with evolving lore.

5.6 PLAYER THEORIES AND COMMUNITY SPECULATION

The Fortnite community often speculates on upcoming events and storylines, creating theories that enrich the experience. Here are some popular theories:

The End of The Loop

Many players believe that The Seven's goal is to break the Loop permanently, freeing the island from the IO's control. Speculation about how this might happen has led to theories about future events where players aid The Seven in dismantling the Loop.

The Future of The Zero Point

Some players theorize that the Zero Point may have deeper connections to other realities and dimensions. This theory suggests that Fortnite's storyline will expand to include even more alternate universes and characters.

Possible Return of Midas

Midas, a fan-favorite character, is rumored to make a return, possibly with new powers or alliances. His previous impact on the storyline has players wondering if he'll play a key role in future events.

The Imagined Order's Secret Goals

While the IO seems focused on controlling the Zero Point, some players believe they have a larger agenda involving the multiverse, possibly connected to other dimensions or powerful forces outside of the current storyline.

5.7 WHAT'S NEXT FOR FORTNITE'S STORYLINE?

Anticipated Developments

With each season, Fortnite's story evolves, introducing new conflicts, characters, and mysteries. Here are some directions the story may take:

- **Further Exploration of The Seven's Origins**: Learning more about each member and their abilities could shed light on their purpose.
- **New Factions**: The introduction of new characters and factions may complicate the conflict over the Zero Point, adding layers to the storyline.
- **The Return of Crossovers with Impactful Stories**: As new crossovers are introduced, they may bring significant changes to the island and deepen the lore of Fortnite's universe.

Live Events and Narrative Progression

Live events continue to push the story forward, and future events will likely involve large-scale battles, dimensional rifts, and perhaps the fate of the Zero Point itself. Players can expect more dramatic events that reshape the island and introduce new story arcs.

Speculations on the Endgame of Fortnite's Story

Many players wonder if Fortnite's storyline will culminate in a climactic showdown between The Seven and the IO, possibly leading to a new chapter or map overhaul. The Zero Point's fate could be central to this climax, potentially altering the island forever.

CHAPTER 6: THE CULTURAL IMPACT OF FORTNITE

6.1 Fortnite's Explosion in Popularity

From Game to Global Phenomenon

Fortnite's popularity transcended gaming almost immediately, capturing the attention of millions worldwide with its unique blend of accessible gameplay, vibrant graphics, and community-centered events. The game attracted a diverse audience, including casual gamers, pro players, and celebrities alike.

Cross-Generational Appeal

Fortnite's cartoonish visuals and free-to-play model made it accessible to both younger players and adults. The game's family-friendly design helped it reach a broad demographic, while its competitive aspect kept serious players engaged.

Social Experience

Beyond gameplay, Fortnite became a space where players could socialize, hang out with friends, and attend virtual events. The community aspect allowed players to forge friendships and create shared experiences in a virtual environment, giving Fortnite a social significance beyond typical online games.

6.2 THE RISE OF FORTNITE STREAMERS AND ESPORTS

Influence of Content Creators

Fortnite quickly became one of the most-watched games on streaming platforms like Twitch and YouTube. Popular streamers like *Ninja*, *Tfue*, and *Nick Eh 30* gained millions of followers by showcasing their Fortnite skills and engaging with viewers.

- **Building Careers in Streaming**: Fortnite helped launch the careers of numerous streamers, turning gaming into a viable profession. Many content creators used Fortnite to establish a platform, creating opportunities for partnerships, sponsorships, and brand deals.
- **Engagement with Viewers**: Streamers brought fans closer to the game, often hosting live events, "watch parties," and interactive streams where viewers could join custom games, participate in Q&A sessions, and watch major events together.

Esports and Competitive Scene

- **The Fortnite World Cup**: The 2019 Fortnite World Cup was a milestone, offering a $30 million prize pool. Thousands of players from around the world participated in qualifiers, and the tournament drew millions of viewers globally.
- **Cash Cups and FNCS**: Epic Games regularly hosts Cash Cups and the Fortnite Champion Series (FNCS),

keeping competitive players engaged with prize pools and points-based leaderboards. These tournaments offer players a chance to prove their skills and gain recognition in the Fortnite community.

6.3 FORTNITE AND MUSIC: VIRTUAL CONCERTS AND BEYOND

Pioneering the In-Game Concert

Fortnite set a new standard for virtual events with in-game concerts, allowing millions of players to attend live performances without leaving the game.

- **The Marshmello Concert (2019)**: This was Fortnite's first major concert, attracting over 10 million players. The event demonstrated Fortnite's potential as a platform for music and entertainment, allowing players to enjoy a digital concert in a shared space.
- **Travis Scott's Astronomical (2020)**: Travis Scott's virtual concert was a visual and musical spectacle, drawing over 12 million concurrent players. The performance featured surreal landscapes, gravity-defying effects, and fan-favorite songs, setting a new standard for interactive digital events.
- **Ariana Grande's Rift Tour (2021)**: Pop icon Ariana Grande performed in an in-game event that took players on a multi-dimensional journey, combining visuals and interactivity. This concert demonstrated Fortnite's versatility as a digital performance space, where music, gaming, and art converge.

Music Partnerships and Collaborations

Fortnite has partnered with numerous artists, featuring exclusive music packs, skins, and emotes based on popular songs. These collaborations allow artists to reach a new audience, and players can celebrate their favorite musicians within the game.

6.4 FORTNITE'S INFLUENCE ON FASHION AND MERCHANDISING

In-Game Skins and Cosmetics

Fortnite's vibrant skins, back bling, and emotes allow players to express their unique style. This customization element became a major draw, with players often collecting exclusive outfits and emotes to personalize their avatars.

- **Icon Series Skins**: Epic Games introduced Icon Series skins, inspired by real-world figures like *Ninja*, *Travis Scott*, and *Lachlan*. These skins give players a chance to emulate their favorite personalities in-game.
- **Seasonal Themes and Unique Looks**: Each season brings a new lineup of skins, often inspired by the season's theme or pop culture trends. From superhero-inspired designs to futuristic suits, these skins encourage players to collect and show off their exclusive looks.

Fashion Collaborations

- **Balenciaga Collaboration**: Fortnite partnered with the high-end fashion brand Balenciaga to create in-game skins and real-world apparel. This crossover blurred the lines between gaming and fashion, appealing to fans of both.

- **Other Fashion Collaborations**: Fortnite has also worked with brands like *Nike* and *Jordan*, releasing limited-edition skins and items inspired by popular brands, which gave players a sense of prestige and exclusivity.

Fortnite Merchandise

The game's popularity led to a wide range of physical merchandise, including action figures, clothing, and even Fortnite-themed toys. This expansion into retail and merchandising allowed Fortnite to establish a strong brand presence outside the digital world.

6.5 FORTNITE AS A SOCIAL PLATFORM

Virtual Hangouts and Party Royale

Fortnite introduced *Party Royale*, a non-combat mode where players can relax, play mini-games, and socialize without the pressure of competition. This mode highlights Fortnite's role as a social platform, giving players a place to hang out with friends in a low-stakes environment.

Social Connection During COVID-19

During the COVID-19 pandemic, Fortnite became a popular way for people to stay connected. With physical gatherings limited, players used Fortnite to interact with friends, participate in virtual events, and attend in-game concerts, providing a sense of normalcy and social interaction.

Political and Educational Events

Fortnite has also hosted events beyond gaming, like the *We the People* discussion on racial justice in America. These events used Fortnite as a platform for education and social awareness, proving that games can serve as spaces for meaningful conversation and learning.

6.6 MEMES, DANCE TRENDS, AND SOCIAL MEDIA IMPACT

The Impact of Emotes and Dance Moves

Fortnite's emotes, especially dance moves, have become iconic and highly recognizable. Many players use these emotes to celebrate victories, joke with friends, or express themselves in unique ways.

- **Popular Dance Trends**: Fortnite introduced dances like *The Floss*, *Orange Justice*, and *Take the L*, which quickly became viral trends on social media platforms like TikTok and Instagram.
- **Memes and Viral Moments**: Fortnite has generated countless memes, from "default dancing" to jokes about popular skins, adding humor and relatability to the game's community.

Social Media Influence

- **Instagram and TikTok**: Many players share clips, memes, and highlights from Fortnite on social media, creating a space where fans can enjoy and share Fortnite content outside the game.
- **User-Generated Content**: Platforms like TikTok and Twitter are full of fan-made Fortnite content, from memes and trick shots to tutorials and dance routines. Fortnite's social media presence allows players to connect with others and showcase their creativity.

6.7 FORTNITE'S IMPACT ON YOUTH CULTURE

Changing the Gaming Landscape for Young Players

Fortnite's free-to-play model and accessible gameplay have made it a popular choice for younger players, many of whom use the game as a primary social space. Its collaborative modes encourage teamwork and interaction, fostering a sense of community.

Influence on Communication

For many young players, Fortnite is their first experience with online social interactions. In-game chat, party modes, and emotes teach basic online etiquette and team dynamics, skills that are increasingly important in digital environments.

Educational Use and Skill Development

Some educators see Fortnite as a tool for teaching various skills, such as critical thinking, teamwork, and strategic planning. For example:

- **Problem-Solving**: Fortnite's building mechanics and combat strategies require players to think quickly and adapt to changing situations.
- **Communication and Teamwork**: In team modes, players learn the importance of clear communication and coordinated effort to achieve success.

6.8 CONTROVERSIES AND CRITICISMS

Concerns Over Screen Time and Addiction

Fortnite's highly engaging gameplay loop has led to concerns about screen time and addiction, especially among younger players. The game's reward system, events, and cosmetic collectibles can create a compulsive loop, making it difficult for some players to moderate their time.

Microtransactions and the Business Model

While Fortnite is free-to-play, it relies heavily on microtransactions for revenue. Players can purchase V-Bucks to buy skins, emotes, and battle passes. While these items don't affect gameplay, some critics argue that the pressure to keep up with new skins can encourage spending, especially among younger players.

Legal Disputes

Fortnite has been involved in legal battles, notably with Apple over in-app purchases. Epic Games sued Apple after Fortnite was removed from the App Store, arguing that Apple's policies were restrictive. This high-profile case brought attention to the relationship between app developers and platform owners, sparking debates on digital monopolies and fair practices.

6.9 FORTNITE'S INFLUENCE ON OTHER GAMES

Popularizing the Battle Pass System

Fortnite popularized the *battle pass* system, a tiered progression model that rewards players with cosmetic items as they level up. Many games, including *Apex Legends*, *Call of Duty: Warzone*, and *Rocket League*, adopted similar models, demonstrating Fortnite's influence on gaming monetization.

Encouraging Crossovers and Collaboration

Fortnite's success with crossovers inspired other games to incorporate similar partnerships, adding popular characters, weapons, and themed events from other franchises. The success of these collaborations shows Fortnite's impact on how games approach in-game content and cultural integration.

Innovating Virtual Events in Gaming

Fortnite's virtual concerts and events have become a model for other games, demonstrating that virtual worlds can serve as stages for music, art, and social gatherings. Titles like *Roblox* and *Minecraft* have adopted similar approaches, hosting in-game events to keep players engaged.

CHAPTER 7: TRAINING TO BECOME A PRO PLAYER

7.1 Building a Practice Routine

The Importance of Consistency

Becoming a professional player requires dedication and a structured approach to practice. Regular, focused practice is essential for skill improvement, as it builds muscle memory, hones reflexes, and strengthens decision-making abilities under pressure.

Creating a Balanced Routine

A well-rounded routine should include building, aiming, editing, and combat drills. Aim to dedicate specific time slots each day to different areas of improvement, while balancing practice with rest to avoid burnout.

Suggested Weekly Practice Schedule

- **Day 1**: Aim and accuracy training (1-2 hours); Creative Mode building drills (1-2 hours)
- **Day 2**: Arena Mode for combat practice (2 hours); editing drills (1-2 hours)
- **Day 3**: Custom scrims with friends or teammates (2-3 hours)
- **Day 4**: Rotations and positioning practice in regular Battle Royale matches (2-3 hours)
- **Day 5**: Creative Mode to focus on high-ground retakes

and box fighting (2-3 hours)
- **Day 6**: Tournament simulation with endgame focus in scrims (2-3 hours)
- **Day 7**: Rest day and VOD review of previous games to identify areas for improvement

This structure provides a mix of solo practice and team play, helping to build well-rounded skills.

7.2 Essential Skills for Competitive Play

Building and Editing

- **Building Skills**: Master key building techniques like 90s, ramp-rushing, and tunneling. These provide you with a foundation for both offense and defense.
- **Editing Skills**: Editing allows you to modify structures for quick peeks, surprise attacks, and defensive resets. Practice edits in Creative Mode until they feel natural and efficient.

Aiming and Precision

- **Tracking vs. Flick Shots**: Fortnite combat requires both steady tracking (following an opponent's movement) and flick shots (quickly aiming at a new target). Training maps in Creative Mode can help improve these skills.
- **Crosshair Placement**: Keep your crosshair at head level when moving and aiming, as this reduces the need for large aim adjustments in fights.

Situational Awareness and Game Sense

- **Awareness of Surroundings**: Stay alert to sounds, structures, and player movements in your vicinity. Using a headset and setting audio cues can improve awareness.
- **Game Sense**: Develop a feel for when to engage, rotate, or avoid fights. Game sense improves with experience,

VOD reviews, and analyzing other high-level players.

7.3 Setting Goals and Tracking Progress

SMART Goals

Set specific, measurable, achievable, relevant, and time-bound (SMART) goals. For example, aim to reach a new rank in Arena Mode within a month or practice high-ground retakes for 30 minutes daily for a week.

Tracking Your Improvement

- **Daily Journal**: Write down key takeaways after each practice session. Include reflections on what went well and what needs improvement.
- **Use of Analytics**: Track stats like kill/death ratios, win rates, and average placement in tournaments. Monitoring these metrics over time shows your progress and highlights areas that need work.

Celebrating Small Wins

Acknowledging small achievements—such as mastering a new building technique or improving accuracy—keeps you motivated and reinforces positive habits.

7.4 Training in Creative Mode

Best Creative Maps for Training

Creative Mode has a variety of player-made maps designed for specific training purposes. Some recommended types include:

- **Aim Trainers**: Practice tracking, flick shots, and precision shooting on maps with moving targets.
- **Edit Courses**: Complete edit courses to improve editing speed and accuracy under time constraints.
- **Building Courses**: Some maps are dedicated to building practice, focusing on high-ground retakes, 90s, and defensive building.
- **Box Fight Arenas**: Practice close-range combat in box fight maps, simulating the high-stakes situations

common in competitive Fortnite.

Custom Training Routines

Create custom routines for Creative Mode to work on specific skills. For example, spend 15 minutes warming up with aim drills, followed by 30 minutes of building practice, and finish with 15 minutes of editing.

Practicing with Friends or Teammates

Training with others can simulate real-match dynamics and help develop teamwork and communication skills. Set up friendly scrims or building challenges to keep practice engaging and competitive.

7.5 Mastering Endgame Situations

Late-Game Strategy and Movement

- **Tunneling**: Use tunnels to move safely in late-game zones where open areas can be dangerous. Focus on quick, efficient builds to save materials.
- **Height Management**: Avoid building too high, as fall damage can be fatal. Build just enough to secure a safe position and maintain visibility.
- **Material Conservation**: Conserve materials for the final circles. Switch between wood, stone, and metal strategically to maintain durability and save resources.

Rotation Techniques

- **Early Rotations**: Move early to avoid congestion and find safe positioning in the new circle.
- **Late Rotations**: Sometimes, moving late can prevent enemies from tracking you, but this requires precise movement and strong awareness of your surroundings.
- **Using Utility Items**: Launch pads, shockwave grenades, and rift-to-go items are essential for quick rotations. Master their use to navigate the storm and avoid enemy fire.

7.6 Scrims and Tournament Preparation

The Role of Scrims

Scrims are custom matches with competitive players, often set up to simulate tournament-style endgames. They offer a chance to practice rotations, material management, and endgame strategy in a high-pressure setting.

Joining Scrims and Communities

- **Discord Servers**: Many Fortnite scrim communities exist on Discord, where players organize practice matches for specific skill levels.
- **Online Tournaments and Cash Cups**: Participate in online tournaments and Cash Cups as a way to gain experience in real competitive settings.

Preparing for a Tournament Day

- **Warm-Up Routine**: Dedicate at least an hour to warming up with aim and building exercises. Review specific strategies with teammates.
- **Mental Preparation**: Practice mindfulness and focus exercises to stay calm under pressure. A clear, focused mindset can help you make better decisions.
- **Nutrition and Rest**: Eat a balanced meal and stay hydrated before a tournament. Avoid caffeine right before playing, as it can increase anxiety or jitteriness.

7.7 Reviewing Gameplay (VOD Review)

Importance of VOD Review

Reviewing your own gameplay (or VOD review) is a critical practice for improvement. By analyzing past matches, you can identify mistakes, spot patterns, and reinforce positive behaviors.

Key Elements to Analyze

- **Positioning Mistakes**: Look for instances where poor positioning led to unnecessary risks or unfavorable engagements.

- **Engagement Choices**: Review decisions to engage or avoid fights, noting if they were strategically sound or if they put you at a disadvantage.
- **Resource Management**: Check your material usage throughout the game, especially in endgame situations. Determine if you could have conserved resources more effectively.

Studying High-Level Players

In addition to reviewing your own gameplay, watch videos of professional players. Analyze their building techniques, combat decisions, and rotations to learn new strategies and improve your own skills.

Peer Feedback

If possible, share your VODs with friends or teammates for feedback. They may spot issues or areas of improvement that you missed. Constructive feedback can provide fresh insights and new ideas.

7.8 Building Mental Resilience and Focus

Dealing with Losses and Setbacks

Competitive Fortnite can be mentally challenging, with inevitable losses and setbacks. To stay motivated:

- **Adopt a Growth Mindset**: View each loss as a learning opportunity. Analyzing mistakes helps turn failures into lessons, keeping you focused on improvement.
- **Avoid Tilt**: Don't let one mistake or bad game impact your performance in the next. Take breaks when necessary to reset your focus.

Maintaining Focus Under Pressure

- **Breathing Techniques**: Practice deep breathing to calm nerves during high-stakes situations, such as the final circles in tournaments.
- **Visualization**: Before matches, visualize different

scenarios and successful outcomes. This helps boost confidence and prepares you mentally for challenges.

- **Positive Self-Talk**: Reinforce positive thinking to build mental resilience. Avoid negative thoughts that can disrupt focus and confidence.

Developing a Support System

Having a support system of friends, family, or teammates can help manage stress and motivation levels. Sharing experiences with others who understand the challenges of competitive gaming can provide emotional support.

7.9 Staying Physically Healthy for Peak Performance

Physical Fitness and Gaming

Physical fitness has a direct impact on performance. Simple exercises can improve reflexes, endurance, and mental clarity.

- **Hand and Eye Exercises**: Stretch your hands and wrists to prevent strain, and practice eye exercises to reduce fatigue from prolonged screen time.
- **Cardio and Aerobic Exercise**: Engaging in regular cardio activities (like jogging or cycling) improves blood flow and energy levels, which support focus during long gaming sessions.
- **Stretching**: Stretching helps maintain flexibility and reduces the risk of strain, especially for the back, shoulders, and neck.

Healthy Eating and Hydration

A balanced diet provides sustained energy, while staying hydrated reduces fatigue. Avoid excessive caffeine, which can cause crashes and jitteriness. Focus on whole foods, protein, and complex carbohydrates for sustained energy.

Balanced Sleep Schedule

Consistent, quality sleep is essential for cognitive function, reaction time, and mental clarity. Aim for 7-8 hours each night to perform your best in training and competitive play.

CHAPTER 8: GAME UPDATES AND THE EVER-EVOLVING META

8.1 Understanding the Meta and Why It Matters

What is the "Meta"?

The "meta" refers to the most effective strategies, weapons, and tactics at any given time. The meta changes frequently as new items are added, others are vaulted, and mechanics are adjusted. Staying aware of the meta is essential for players who want to remain competitive.

How the Meta Affects Gameplay

A shift in the meta can influence everything from optimal loadouts and building styles to combat strategies and rotations. When new weapons or mechanics are introduced, they can redefine what players prioritize, making it important to adapt quickly.

Types of Meta Shifts

- **Seasonal Changes**: Each new season typically brings a major meta shift with map changes, new weapons, and gameplay mechanics.
- **Patch Updates**: Smaller patches introduce balance adjustments and new items, leading to mini meta shifts that can affect gameplay at a granular level.
- **Community Discoveries**: Sometimes, players discover techniques or weapon combinations that change the

meta, like the "Double Pump" or "Ramp Rush." These strategies often spread quickly and can impact player behavior.

8.2 Adapting to New Weapons and Items

Evaluating New Weapons

When a new weapon is introduced, try it out in Creative Mode or unranked matches to understand its strengths and weaknesses. Determine if it fills a unique role in your loadout or if it's worth incorporating into your strategy.

Understanding Weapon Balancing

Fortnite frequently makes small adjustments to weapon stats, such as damage, fire rate, and reload speed. Keep an eye on patch notes to stay informed about these changes and adjust your loadout accordingly.

Utility Items and Their Strategic Uses

Items like grenades, launch pads, and healing items often play a crucial role in the meta. As new utility items are introduced, experiment with how they complement your current strategies and help you navigate difficult situations in matches.

8.3 Adapting to Map Changes

How Map Changes Impact Strategy

With each season, the Fortnite map undergoes transformations that impact popular landing spots, rotation paths, and high-ground areas. Map changes often bring new points of interest (POIs) with unique loot, challenges, and gameplay dynamics.

Learning New Points of Interest (POIs)

- **Exploring New Locations**: Spend time exploring new POIs to understand their layout, loot distribution, and choke points. This knowledge is critical for deciding where to land and how to navigate the area during engagements.
- **High-Traffic Areas**: Some POIs become popular

landing spots due to their loot density or positioning. Knowing these areas helps you decide when to engage or avoid high-risk encounters.

Adjusting Your Rotations

Map changes can disrupt established rotation paths, making it necessary to adapt. Reassess your usual rotations based on the new map layout, especially if your go-to spots have been altered or removed.

8.4 Staying Updated on Patch Notes

Why Patch Notes Matter

Epic Games releases detailed patch notes for each update, highlighting adjustments to weapons, items, and map changes. Reviewing patch notes allows players to understand what has changed and prepare for how these adjustments might influence their strategy.

Identifying Key Changes

Focus on the aspects of the patch notes that directly impact your playstyle:

- **Weapon Adjustments**: Look for changes to damage, range, and reload time for your favorite weapons.
- **Vaulted and Unvaulted Items**: Items can be temporarily removed or reintroduced, affecting available loadouts.
- **Gameplay Mechanics**: Sometimes, Epic Games tweaks movement, building, or combat mechanics, which can significantly alter player strategies.

Staying Informed via Social Media and Communities

Follow Epic Games and Fortnite news accounts on social media to get immediate updates. Many communities, like Reddit and Discord, also provide breakdowns and discussions on how each patch might affect gameplay.

8.5 Testing New Strategies in Creative Mode

Using Creative Mode to Experiment
Creative Mode is an excellent environment for testing new strategies and techniques based on recent updates. For example, you can practice with newly added weapons, build structures to adapt to map changes, or rehearse movement patterns in high-traffic areas.

Simulating Combat Scenarios
Invite friends or join custom matches in Creative Mode to simulate in-game scenarios with new items or mechanics. This practice helps you develop muscle memory and understand how recent changes affect combat dynamics.

Developing Counter-Strategies
When new mechanics or weapons dominate the meta, Creative Mode allows you to experiment with counter-strategies. For example, if a new weapon becomes overpowered, you can practice ways to counter it effectively, helping you adapt and maintain a competitive edge.

8.6 Analyzing Trends in the Meta

Recognizing Patterns in the Meta
Over time, you'll start to notice recurring trends. For instance, certain types of weapons may become powerful at the start of a season, while other items take prominence toward the end. Recognizing these patterns can help you predict and prepare for upcoming shifts.

Following Professional Players
Many pro players analyze and adapt to the meta early, offering insights into effective strategies. Watching high-level gameplay or studying pro players on Twitch or YouTube can reveal emerging trends and advanced techniques that you can incorporate into your own playstyle.

Leveraging Community Insights
Participate in discussions on Reddit, Twitter, and Discord to hear what other players are noticing about the meta. Sometimes,

community members discover powerful weapon combinations or strategies before they become widely known.

8.7 Meta Shifts and Personal Playstyle

Adapting the Meta to Fit Your Playstyle
Not every meta shift requires a drastic change in how you play. If a new weapon or mechanic doesn't complement your style, focus on maintaining your strengths while incorporating smaller adjustments.

Strengthening Core Skills
Regardless of the meta, core skills like building, editing, and aiming remain essential. By continuously honing these abilities, you'll remain adaptable and effective, even as specific tactics or weapons change.

Balancing Playstyle Flexibility with Consistency
While it's important to adapt, having a consistent playstyle helps you build confidence and efficiency in high-pressure situations. Balance flexibility with familiarity, allowing yourself to experiment without losing sight of what works best for you.

8.8 Predictions for Future Meta Shifts

Understanding Seasonal Patterns
Epic Games often introduces major changes at the start of new seasons, such as:

- **New Weapon Classes**: Each season may introduce new types of weapons that alter combat dynamics.
- **Thematic Changes**: Seasonal themes, like superheroes or holiday events, often influence the types of items and POIs on the map.
- **Gameplay Mechanic Updates**: Epic frequently adds or removes mechanics (such as redeploying gliders or using vehicles) to keep gameplay fresh.

Preparing for Likely Changes
Based on previous patterns, here are some changes to anticipate:

- **New Map Layouts**: Be prepared for major changes to the map, possibly adding or removing locations or biomes.
- **Item and Weapon Adjustments**: Assume that popular items may be vaulted or nerfed, while underused items might receive buffs.
- **Environmental Hazards**: Each season may bring unique environmental elements, like floods, earthquakes, or storms, affecting player mobility and positioning.

Adapting Quickly to Meta Shifts

Prepare yourself mentally for change and practice being open to adjusting your loadouts, rotations, and strategies. Staying adaptable allows you to maintain a competitive edge, even if your usual approach needs to be altered.

8.9 The Future of Fortnite and Long-Term Meta Trends

Fortnite's Evolution as a Game

As Fortnite continues to evolve, the game's meta will likely shift toward more complex and diverse strategies. Epic Games shows a commitment to innovation, regularly introducing new content and experiences that challenge players to adapt.

Possible Long-Term Trends

- **Increased Crossovers and Unique Items**: As Fortnite continues to collaborate with franchises, expect new items with unique mechanics that could shake up the meta.
- **Expansion of Mobility Options**: Fortnite may add more vehicles, movement abilities, or mobility items to increase player versatility.
- **Emphasis on Competitive Balance**: Epic may introduce more balancing changes to keep the game fair, especially in competitive modes, as Fortnite's esports scene continues to grow.

Staying Ahead of the Curve

For dedicated players, maintaining an open mindset and eagerness to learn will keep you prepared for Fortnite's evolving landscape. Fortnite's future promises a constantly shifting environment, encouraging players to remain adaptable and creative with their strategies.

CHAPTER 9: THE FUTURE OF FORTNITE

9.1 Fortnite's Role in the Gaming Industry

A Leader in Live-Service Games

Fortnite has set the standard for live-service games by consistently delivering fresh content, seasonal updates, and high-quality events. Its success has influenced other games to adopt similar models, making Fortnite a trailblazer in this space.

Epic's Vision for Fortnite's Future

Epic Games views Fortnite as more than just a game—it's a social platform, an esports title, and a cultural phenomenon. As a flagship property, Fortnite will likely continue to be a focus for innovation and experimentation, whether through new mechanics, crossover events, or community engagement.

Expanding the Fortnite Ecosystem

Epic Games has expanded the Fortnite universe beyond the game, with merchandise, comic book collaborations, and spin-off media. This broadening of the Fortnite brand may continue, with Epic possibly exploring animated series, movies, or even more interactive experiences.

9.2 Anticipated Gameplay Changes

New Mechanics and Items

Epic Games is known for introducing unique items and mechanics that add variety to the gameplay. Potential additions could include:

- **Enhanced Mobility Items**: More options for movement and travel, such as gliders with unique effects, teleportation devices, or grappling tools, could increase strategic possibilities.
- **Dynamic Environmental Effects**: Weather changes, earthquakes, or other environmental hazards could add new challenges, forcing players to adapt their strategies based on changing conditions.

Evolving Building and Editing Mechanics
As players continue to master Fortnite's building and editing systems, Epic may introduce advanced options, like customizable materials or interactive traps, adding depth to construction and combat strategies.

Augmented Reality (AR) and Virtual Reality (VR)
With advances in VR and AR technology, Fortnite could integrate VR support for an immersive experience. Imagine exploring the Fortnite island in first-person VR or using AR to bring Fortnite characters and elements into the real world.

9.3 Possible Future Events and Collaborations

Crossovers with New Universes
Fortnite's crossover events have proven highly popular, so it's likely Epic Games will continue collaborating with other franchises. Potential crossovers might include:

- **Popular Anime Franchises**: Collaborations with well-known anime series like *Naruto* or *Dragon Ball* could attract anime fans and offer unique skins, items, and abilities.
- **Major Movie Releases**: Fortnite could align its crossovers with blockbuster movie releases, introducing themed events and items that coincide with new films.
- **Musical Experiences**: Building on the success of past concerts, Fortnite might host virtual festivals, with

multiple artists performing over a series of nights, creating a true digital music festival experience.

In-Game Narrative Events

Epic Games has continually upped the ante with live events that shape Fortnite's story. Future events might include:

- **Dimensional Rifts and Time Travel**: Players might explore alternate timelines or travel back to previous seasons, experiencing past maps and mechanics in a limited-time event.
- **Player-Driven Storylines**: Interactive events where players can vote or make choices that impact the storyline, creating a dynamic, player-influenced narrative.
- **Larger-Scale Multiplayer Events**: Epic may introduce massive in-game events involving thousands of players on a larger map, making for an unprecedented experience in online gaming.

9.4 Fortnite and the Metaverse

Fortnite as a Metaverse Platform

Epic Games has been vocal about its vision for Fortnite as a metaverse—a shared, persistent virtual space where users can interact, socialize, and create. Fortnite's Creative Mode and Party Royale serve as early examples of Fortnite's potential as a social platform beyond gaming.

The Role of User-Generated Content (UGC)

User-generated content will likely play a key role in Fortnite's evolution into a metaverse. Epic could expand Creative Mode, allowing players to design custom maps, games, and events with more advanced tools.

- **Monetization of UGC**: Epic may introduce systems where creators can monetize their content, incentivizing players to develop high-quality maps, skins, and experiences.

- **Collaboration Spaces**: Fortnite might incorporate dedicated areas for virtual meetings, classes, and social gatherings, making it a multifunctional space for both play and productivity.

Virtual Economies and Digital Ownership
As Fortnite continues to evolve, Epic Games may explore blockchain technology or NFTs, allowing players to truly own digital assets like skins, emotes, or custom maps. This shift could create a virtual economy where players trade and sell their in-game items.

9.5 Fortnite's Future in Esports

Evolving Tournament Formats
Fortnite esports will likely continue to grow, with Epic experimenting with new formats and structures to keep competitions fresh and accessible.

- **Team-Based Competitions**: Epic might introduce official teams or guilds, allowing for large-scale team-based events that go beyond traditional Duos or Trios.
- **Seasonal and Thematic Tournaments**: Themed tournaments tied to each season's story could add an extra layer of engagement, encouraging players to follow both the storyline and esports events.
- **Regional Leagues**: Epic could introduce regional leagues, giving players the chance to compete at local, national, and international levels, similar to professional sports leagues.

The Role of VR and AR in Esports
With VR technology advancing, Fortnite esports could eventually include a VR component, creating a more immersive and spectator-friendly experience. VR viewers could watch matches from within the Fortnite environment, bringing a new dimension to esports broadcasting.

New Spectator Experiences

Epic may introduce enhanced spectator modes, where fans can watch tournaments from unique perspectives, such as first-person view, top-down views, or even through interactive, guided tours. These changes could make esports more engaging and accessible for audiences.

9.6 Predictions for the Fortnite Community

An Increasingly Diverse Player Base

As Fortnite expands its game modes, it will likely attract even more diverse audiences. With a mix of casual social spaces, competitive events, and creative tools, Fortnite could become a game that appeals to all ages and interests.

More Influential Content Creators

With Fortnite's ongoing popularity, the game will continue to be a launchpad for content creators. As new tools, cosmetics, and gameplay options are introduced, creators will have endless material for streams, tutorials, and challenges.

Continued Growth of Online Communities

Fortnite's social media presence and online communities will likely grow, with fans discussing updates, theories, and gameplay tips. Dedicated forums and Discord communities could become even more specialized, covering topics like map-building, competitive tips, and lore analysis.

9.7 Fortnite's Cultural Impact and Legacy

Defining Gaming Trends

Fortnite has already influenced numerous gaming trends, from battle passes to live events. In the future, Fortnite may continue to shape the gaming industry by experimenting with virtual concerts, fashion crossovers, and innovative content creation.

The Legacy of Fortnite as a Social Platform

Fortnite's impact goes beyond gaming; it has become a cultural touchstone and a pioneer in the virtual social space. Its success with in-game concerts, charity events, and interactive storylines will likely inspire future games to follow its lead, integrating social elements into gaming experiences.

Fortnite as a Model for Future Games

Fortnite's ongoing innovation has set a high bar for other developers, who now see the potential for games to evolve and adapt. Fortnite's ability to maintain relevance and excitement over years could serve as a model for future live-service games.

9.8 Fortnite's Potential as an Educational Tool

Learning Through Gaming

With its growing focus on Creative Mode and interactive experiences, Fortnite could evolve as an educational platform, where players can learn through gaming. Potential educational applications include:

- **STEM Learning Modules**: Creative Mode could host mini-games and puzzles that teach math, physics, and engineering concepts.
- **History and Culture Lessons**: Fortnite's vast, flexible world could be used to create historical or cultural simulations, where players explore past events or other cultures.

Educational Partnerships

Fortnite could partner with schools, museums, or educational organizations to develop learning-focused content. Imagine a museum tour within Fortnite or a science-themed scavenger hunt designed in collaboration with educators.

Digital Citizenship and Online Interaction

As an interactive social space, Fortnite offers opportunities to teach digital citizenship. Players could learn about online etiquette, collaboration, and critical thinking, preparing younger audiences for positive interactions in the digital world.

9.9 Looking Ahead: Fortnite's Long-Term Future

Continuous Evolution as a Game and Platform

Epic Games has shown a commitment to evolving Fortnite, so players can expect it to continue changing over the years. Whether through gameplay innovations, cross-platform expansions, or metaverse ambitions, Fortnite will likely remain a key player in the gaming world.

Speculations on Fortnite's Ultimate Endgame

As the storyline progresses, some players speculate that Fortnite may eventually reach a climactic event or narrative conclusion. However, given the game's success and potential, Epic is more likely to keep the story going, introducing new dimensions, characters, and challenges as time goes on.

Fortnite's Enduring Impact on Gaming

Regardless of what the future holds, Fortnite's influence on gaming is undeniable. It has redefined the possibilities for interactive experiences, multiplayer gaming, and virtual events. As Fortnite continues to evolve, its legacy will remain as a landmark in gaming history.

CHAPTER 10: THE LASTING LEGACY OF FORTNITE

10.1 Fortnite's Cultural Significance

A Global Phenomenon

Fortnite's impact extends beyond the gaming community, influencing pop culture, fashion, music, and entertainment. It has become a staple of modern culture, with its dances, memes, and in-game events recognized worldwide.

A Platform for Connection

Fortnite redefined the online multiplayer experience by creating a virtual space for connection. Through its interactive events, concerts, and crossovers, Fortnite has become a social platform where players can connect, celebrate, and share experiences together.

Fortnite's Reach Across Generations

Unlike many games that appeal to a single demographic, Fortnite has captivated players of all ages. Families play together, friends meet up in-game, and Fortnite bridges generational gaps, appealing to everyone from young players to adults.

10.2 The Impact on the Gaming Industry

The Rise of Live-Service Models

Fortnite popularized the live-service model, inspiring other games to adopt frequent updates, seasonal content, and ongoing community engagement. Its success demonstrated the potential of games to evolve and remain relevant through constant innovation.

Inspiration for New Games and Genres

Fortnite's success has spurred countless games in the battle royale genre, influencing titles like *Apex Legends*, *Call of Duty: Warzone*, and *PUBG*. Beyond battle royales, Fortnite's live events and crossovers inspired games across genres to incorporate social and interactive elements.

Advancements in Cross-Platform Play

Fortnite pushed for cross-platform play, allowing friends on different consoles, PCs, and even mobile devices to play together seamlessly. This move set a new standard in gaming, encouraging other developers to prioritize cross-platform compatibility.

10.3 Fortnite's Influence on Social Media and Pop Culture

Memes, Trends, and Emotes

Fortnite's emotes, dances, and iconic characters have permeated social media, with players creating and sharing content that reaches millions. From viral dances to humorous memes, Fortnite has become a source of online trends that shape digital culture.

The Influence of Streaming and Content Creation

The game's popularity has turned streamers and content creators into celebrities, with players like *Ninja*, *Tfue*, and *Pokimane* amassing millions of followers. Fortnite helped mainstream streaming as a career, demonstrating the power of gaming content in the digital age.

Fortnite's Role in Music and Entertainment

Fortnite's in-game concerts redefined the music experience, drawing millions of players to witness events like the Travis Scott and Ariana Grande concerts. These concerts bridged the gap between music and gaming, creating a new way for fans to engage with artists and musicians.

10.4 Lessons Learned from Fortnite's Evolution

The Importance of Adaptability

Fortnite's ongoing success is rooted in its ability to adapt to trends, listen to community feedback, and reinvent itself. Players and developers alike can learn from Fortnite's willingness to evolve, embracing change as a way to stay relevant and engaging.

Creating Community-Driven Experiences

Epic Games understands the power of community and has involved players in shaping Fortnite's journey. By creating a collaborative atmosphere and offering platforms for feedback, Fortnite has taught the industry the value of community-driven content.

Setting High Standards for Quality

Fortnite's commitment to high-quality graphics, engaging gameplay, and innovative features has set a new standard for gaming. By constantly pushing the boundaries of what's possible, Fortnite has shown that investing in quality can lead to lasting success.

Balancing Business and Player Experience

Although Fortnite is free-to-play, its cosmetic items, battle passes, and microtransactions have generated significant revenue without affecting gameplay balance. Fortnite's monetization strategy demonstrates the importance of balancing profitability with a fair, enjoyable experience for players.

10.5 The Impact of Fortnite on Players

Encouraging Creativity

Fortnite's Creative Mode empowers players to design their own maps, games, and experiences, fostering creativity within the community. Many young players have developed a passion for design and coding through Fortnite's tools, making it a platform for learning and imagination.

Developing Social Skills

For many young players, Fortnite serves as a space for social interaction, teaching teamwork, communication, and digital etiquette. Through cooperative gameplay, players learn valuable skills that extend beyond the game.

Building Competitive Mindsets

Fortnite's competitive modes and tournaments encourage players to develop resilience, perseverance, and a desire for improvement. The competitive environment fosters a growth mindset, teaching players to learn from losses and celebrate achievements.

Creating Lasting Friendships

Fortnite has become a space where friendships flourish, with players meeting, bonding, and sharing experiences in the game. For many, Fortnite is more than just a game—it's a place where real connections are formed.

10.6 What Fortnite Teaches About the Future of Gaming

Gaming as a Platform for Entertainment and Social Interaction

Fortnite has shown that games can be platforms for a variety of experiences beyond gameplay. Whether through concerts, movie screenings, or social hubs like Party Royale, Fortnite demonstrates the potential for games to serve as multifunctional platforms.

Pioneering the Metaverse Concept

Fortnite is at the forefront of the "metaverse" movement— a shared, persistent virtual space where players can socialize, create, and engage. Fortnite's future may continue to explore this concept, leading the way toward more immersive, interactive digital worlds.

Inspiration for Inclusive, Global Gaming Experiences

Fortnite's diverse audience and cross-platform approach demonstrate the power of inclusivity in gaming. As technology advances, the future of gaming will likely prioritize accessibility, creating inclusive experiences that bring players together from all over the world.

10.7 Final Reflections and the Future of Fortnite

A Game That Continues to Evolve

Fortnite's ability to stay relevant through continuous innovation has established it as a model for the industry. The game's evolution shows that, with creativity and adaptability, a game can thrive for years while remaining engaging and exciting.

Fortnite's Legacy in Gaming History

Fortnite's impact on gaming, pop culture, and entertainment will endure. From redefining online interaction to shaping digital experiences, Fortnite has earned its place as a milestone in gaming history.

Looking to the Future

While Fortnite's exact path remains uncertain, one thing is clear: it will continue to innovate, entertain, and connect players. Whether through new gameplay mechanics, immersive events, or expanded social features, Fortnite's journey is far from over, and its legacy will continue to inspire players and developers for years to come.

CHAPTER 11: PLAYER RESOURCES AND INTERACTIVE TOOLS

11.1 Illustrated Guides and Diagrams

Building Techniques Illustrated

- **Step-by-Step Diagrams for Key Builds**: Include visuals for essential builds like 90s, box fighting, and ramp-rush strategies. Each diagram can show the sequence from initial placement to completed structure.
- **Defensive and Offensive Builds**: Illustrate the differences in defensive and offensive builds, highlighting how to use structures for both protection and attack.
- **High-Ground Retake Techniques**: Visual examples of retakes, including side ramps, cone placements, and layered defenses.

Map and Rotations Diagrams

- **Popular Points of Interest (POIs)**: Maps that showcase key landing spots and high-traffic areas, with notes on loot availability and tactical advantages.
- **Safe Rotations and Hot Zones**: Highlight rotation routes that balance safety with resource gathering, showing the advantages of each path based on typical storm patterns.

Weapon and Loadout Comparisons

- **Weapon Stats and Loadout Options**: Infographics comparing stats like fire rate, damage, and reload speed. Display ideal loadouts for different scenarios (e.g., close-quarters, mid-range, long-range).
- **Healing and Utility Item Guide**: Visual guide to healing and utility items, with recommendations on when and how to use each item effectively.

The 90:
A Comprehensive Guide

MASTERING THE 90-DEGREE TURN IN BUILDING

The **90-degree turn**, often just called "90s," is a fundamental building technique for players seeking rapid vertical movement. By combining quick turns and precise building placements, 90s allow players to gain height efficiently—a significant advantage in Fortnite. The technique involves rotating 90 degrees to maintain forward momentum while ascending quickly, leveraging structures like ramps, walls, and floors for support. Since controlling the high ground often leads to victory, mastering the 90s is an essential skill.

What is a "90"?

A 90 is essentially a rapid upward-building sequence that relies on constructing a ramp alongside strategically placed walls and floors. This method involves quick movements to create turns, allowing players to ascend without losing speed or control. Each 90 sequence can be linked seamlessly with another, meaning players can stack multiple 90s to build towers swiftly.

Basic Technique: To perform a 90:

1. Start on a ramp, ensuring that there's enough headroom above you.
2. Turn 90 degrees and construct walls to secure your structure.
3. Place a new ramp to maintain your upward

momentum.

The technique can vary slightly in how many walls or floors are used, which affects both material cost and protection.

Common Variants:

1. **Clockwise and Counterclockwise 90s**: Players turn in either direction, placing walls in a circular pattern for added stability. Clockwise turns generally require less mouse movement, while counterclockwise turns add additional wall coverage, providing protection on specific sides.

2. **Two-Wall 90s**: A more material-efficient method that only places walls on two sides instead of fully enclosing the structure. This approach is faster but offers less cover.

3. **Floorless 90s**: Omits floors to save materials, using only ramps and walls to achieve the 90-degree rotation. This version is best suited for players comfortable with rapid, high-precision movements.

ADVANCED 90 TECHNIQUES

Sequential 90s: Most players can chain up to three 90s without jump fatigue becoming an issue. As fatigue sets in, players may consider transitioning to a different approach or taking advantage of no-jump or anti-jump techniques.

1. **No-Jump 90s**: Skip the jump and rely on ramp placement alone. This technique minimizes fatigue, allowing for more extended building sequences.

2. **Anti-Jump Fatigue 90s**: By briefly pausing between turns, players can reset jump fatigue, allowing for consecutive, effective jumps.

CHOOSING THE RIGHT 90 FOR YOUR PLAYSTYLE

Each 90 variant has strengths and trade-offs:

- **Protection-Oriented 90s**: Adding extra walls or a backboard wall increases defense but uses more materials.
- **Speed-Focused 90s**: For faster, efficient builds, use two-wall or floorless 90s.
- **Control-Focused 90s**: No-jump and anti-jump options are ideal for maintaining control over height without jump fatigue.

By practicing these variations, players can adapt to different combat scenarios, whether they need quick height, robust cover, or efficient material use. With enough practice, 90s become a reflexive skill, allowing players to dominate in vertical gameplay.

Defensive vs. Offensive Builds

Defensive Builds: Defensive builds focus on protection, allowing players to shield themselves from enemy attacks, recover health, or reposition safely. These builds prioritize coverage and resilience, often incorporating enclosed structures that give players time to reload, plan, or heal.

Key Defensive Techniques:

1. **Boxing Up**: Construct a quick 1x1 box (walls, floor,

and roof) to protect yourself from all sides. This build is effective when under heavy fire and provides a safe spot to regroup.

2. **Layered Walls**: Placing double layers of walls on the side facing opponents can increase durability and delay damage. This tactic is ideal for countering strong attacks or snipers.

3. **Cone and Roof Edits**: Adding cones or roofs inside the box allows players to edit and create peeking windows, allowing for controlled, low-risk shots at opponents.

4. **Extended Tunneling**: Defensive tunneling allows players to move forward while remaining protected on all sides. This is especially useful in the late game to avoid exposure.

HIGH-GROUND RETAKE TECHNIQUES

High-ground retakes are essential for gaining a strategic advantage in Fortnite, especially during close-quarters or late-game fights. These techniques help players regain or maintain height over opponents, giving them visibility and control of the battlefield. Here are some of the most effective high-ground retake techniques, each using specific structures and placements to block opponents, protect the player, and build upward efficiently.

1. Side Ramp Retake

The side ramp technique involves building ramps along the side of an opponent's structure, enabling players to ascend while keeping their position protected from enemy fire.

Steps:

- Place a ramp leading up to the side of the opponent's structure.
- Build walls along the outer edge of the ramp for additional cover.
- Continue placing ramps and walls as you advance upward.

2. Cone and Ramp Layering

This technique uses cones placed above ramps to block an opponent's progress, forcing them to slow down or reroute. Cones prevent opponents from building directly over the player, providing a brief advantage to continue upward.

Steps:

- Start with a ramp and immediately place a cone above the ramp to block the opponent.
- Continue building upward by layering another ramp, repeating cone placement above.
- For added security, place walls around the ramp-cone structure to prevent enemies from shooting through.

3. Layered Defense with Double Ramps

Layered defense combines multiple ramps with walls and floors to protect against enemy shots while moving up quickly. This technique is especially useful for high-stakes endgame situations when multiple players may be targeting the same high ground.

Steps:

- Begin with two ramps placed side-by-side to create a wider base.

- Add walls along the outer edges of both ramps to prevent shots from hitting the player.
- Place floors and cones on top of the ramps for added layers of defense, making it harder for opponents to shoot through.

4. 180-Degree Turn Retake

This technique involves a quick 180-degree turn to reposition and continue ascending, blocking the opponent's view and creating an unexpected angle.

Steps:

- Place a ramp and walls as usual while moving upward.
- Turn 180 degrees and immediately place another ramp in the opposite direction, followed by walls.
- Repeat this sequence as you continue ascending to confuse the opponent and make it harder for them to predict your movement.

5. Triple Edit Retake with Cone Placement

The triple edit involves placing cones and walls in a pattern that allows quick edits to maintain momentum while ascending. It's effective for blocking an opponent's view and gaining high ground rapidly.

Steps:

- Begin with a ramp and place cones and walls in front and to the sides.
- Use quick edits on the cones and walls to create openings for upward movement.
- Continue placing cones and walls, using edits to maintain a clear path while keeping structures intact to prevent shots from the opponent.

SUMMARY DIAGRAM: HIGH-GROUND RETAKE TECHNIQUES COMPARISON

To further clarify each technique, a summary diagram can highlight each retake side-by-side. This allows readers to compare:

- **Protection Level**: Visual indicators showing walls, ramps, and cones for cover.
- **Speed and Efficiency**: Icons or text showing which techniques are fastest for quick height gains.
- **Best Situations for Use**: Labels indicating when each technique is best applied (e.g., early-game, close-quarters, or endgame).

11.2 Player Exercises and Practice Drills

Weekly Practice Routines

- **Day-by-Day Schedule**: A suggested weekly training schedule for practicing specific skills (e.g., building drills on Mondays, aiming exercises on Tuesdays).
- **Creative Mode Challenges**: Challenges designed to build specific skills, like editing speed, aiming accuracy, or high-ground retakes.

Skill-Building Drills

- **Aiming Drills**: Exercises like tracking moving targets, practicing flick shots, and improving crosshair placement. Include recommended Creative maps for targeting and shooting practice.

- **Building and Editing Drills**: Drills to practice box fights, 90s, piece control, and editing resets. Include time-based challenges to improve speed and accuracy.
- **Endgame Simulations**: Practice routines for simulating endgame situations, such as tunneling, rotating in small zones, and material conservation.

11.3 Case Studies and Pro Play Examples

Tournament Play Analysis

- **Iconic Tournament Moments**: Breakdown of memorable plays from pro tournaments, explaining the player's decision-making, positioning, and building techniques.
- **In-Depth Look at Popular Pro Tactics**: Analyze tactics used by top players, like advanced rotation strategies or double ramp-rush techniques, and explain how to apply these strategies.

Detailed Example of Endgame Strategy

- **Endgame Simulation Case Study**: Provide an example of an endgame scenario with step-by-step explanations of player choices, including when to build, rotate, and engage.
- **Materials and Resources Case Study**: Illustrate how a pro player manages materials in high-pressure situations, explaining when and how to conserve resources effectively.

11.4 Glossary of Fortnite Terms

ESSENTIAL TERMS FOR NEW PLAYERS

Battle Royale Vocabulary

1. **Storm Circle**: The area on the map that players must stay within as the match progresses. The storm circle shrinks over time, and players outside the circle will take damage from the storm.

2. **High Ground**: The elevated position in a fight. Gaining the high ground gives players a visibility and strategic advantage, as it's easier to spot and attack opponents below.

3. **Piece Control**: Controlling and placing builds around an opponent to limit their movement. By editing and placing walls, floors, and ramps strategically, players can trap opponents or force them into vulnerable positions.

4. **Zone Rotation**: Moving from one area of the map to another to stay within the safe zone (storm circle) as it shrinks. Effective zone rotation helps players avoid unnecessary fights and find optimal positioning.

5. **Drop Spot**: The location where players choose to land at the start of the match. Good drop spots have high-quality loot and limited enemy presence, giving players a strong start.

6. **Late Game**: The final stages of the match when the storm circle is small, and most players are in close

proximity. Building skills and positioning are crucial in this phase.

7. **Revive**: In team modes, downed teammates can be revived to bring them back into the game. Reviving takes a few seconds and can be interrupted by enemy attacks.

8. **Supply Drop**: A crate that falls from the sky at random locations during the game, containing high-level weapons and healing items. Supply drops are highly contested because of their valuable contents.

Weapon and Item Glossary

1. **Assault Rifle (AR)**: A versatile, mid-range weapon useful in various situations. ARs are balanced in fire rate, damage, and range, making them popular for all types of players.

2. **Shotgun**: A close-range weapon with high damage, ideal for quick eliminations in close encounters. Shotguns are effective in box fights and building combat.

3. **Sniper Rifle**: A long-range weapon with high damage, ideal for picking off enemies from a distance. Snipers require precision and can deal one-shot eliminations with headshots.

4. **Submachine Gun (SMG)**: A rapid-fire weapon with a high fire rate, useful for close-range combat. SMGs are often used in combination with shotguns to finish off opponents.

5. **Rocket Launcher**: A heavy weapon that fires explosive rockets, dealing splash damage in a small radius. Rocket launchers are effective for breaking structures and forcing opponents out of cover.

6. **Healing Items**:

- **Medkit**: Restores a player's health to 100. It takes 10 seconds to use, so it's best applied in safe areas.
- **Mini Shield**: A quick-use shield item that grants 25 shield points, up to a maximum of 50 shield.
- **Big Shield (Shield Potion)**: Grants 50 shield points and can be stacked up to 100.
- **Bandages**: Basic healing items that restore small amounts of health but can only heal up to 75% of total health.

7. **Utility Items**:
    - **Launch Pad**: A deployable pad that launches players into the air, allowing for quick movement across the map or escaping fights.
    - **Shockwave Grenade**: An explosive that pushes players in a specific direction without causing damage. Useful for fast movement or rotating to the safe zone.
    - **Chug Splash**: A throwable healing item that provides a small amount of health and shield to both the player and nearby teammates.

8. **Rarities**:
    - **Common** (Gray): Basic-level weapons with standard stats.
    - **Uncommon** (Green): Slightly improved weapons with higher stats.
    - **Rare** (Blue): Higher-quality weapons with increased damage or accuracy.
    - **Epic** (Purple): Powerful weapons with advanced stats, often rare to find.
    - **Legendary** (Gold): Top-tier weapons with the best stats and effects.

COMMONLY USED SLANG AND ABBREVIATIONS

Fortnite Slang

1. **Cracked**: Refers to a player who has sustained heavy damage, usually with their shield broken. For example, "He's cracked!" indicates an enemy is low on health and vulnerable.

2. **Third-Party**: Joining an ongoing fight between two other players or teams to take advantage of their weakened state. Third-partying is common in Fortnite as it allows for easy eliminations.

3. **Sweat**: A highly skilled player who plays aggressively and uses advanced building techniques. Sweats are known for their fast, high-pressure playstyles.

4. **Box Fight**: A close-range fight within a confined space, often inside player-built structures. Box fights rely on building and editing skills to control the fight.

5. **Loot**: Items collected around the map, including weapons, healing items, and materials. Players collect loot to improve their chances of winning.

6. **Push**: Moving toward an enemy with the intent to engage in combat, usually after weakening them or gaining an advantage.

7. **One-Shot**: Refers to a player who is so low on health that they can be eliminated with a single hit.

8. **Clutch**: Successfully completing a challenging situation, such as winning a 1v2 or 1v3 scenario. A clutch moment often involves impressive skill or quick decision-making.

Community Abbreviations

1. **GG (Good Game)**: A term used at the end of a match to show sportsmanship and respect toward opponents, regardless of outcome.

2. **LTM (Limited-Time Mode)**: A temporary game mode introduced for a limited period. LTMs vary in gameplay and offer unique challenges or mechanics.

3. **FNCS (Fortnite Champion Series)**: Fortnite's main competitive event, where players compete in various rounds for a chance to win cash prizes and other rewards.

4. **DPS (Damage per Second)**: The amount of damage a weapon deals per second, often used to compare weapons' effectiveness.

5. **KD (Kill/Death Ratio)**: A statistic measuring the average number of eliminations a player gets compared to their own deaths, indicating their overall skill level.

6. **HP (Health Points)**: A measure of a player's life in-game. When HP reaches zero, the player is eliminated.

7. **AFK (Away from Keyboard)**: Refers to players who are inactive or unresponsive. "AFK" players may have stepped away from the game temporarily.

8. **POI (Point of Interest)**: Designated locations on the map with notable features and loot, such as named areas or popular landmarks.

11.5 Player Interviews and Stories

1. Competitive Player Profile: Max "Blitz" Carter
Age: **17**
Playstyle: **Aggressive, High-Ground Specialist**
Favorite Weapon: **Pump Shotgun**
Favorite Drop Spot: **Lazy Lake**

Interview:

Q: Can you tell us about your daily training routine?
A: Sure! I usually start with an hour in Creative Mode for warm-up. I'll do 90s, building drills, and edit courses to get my speed and accuracy down. After that, I'll spend about an hour practicing aim using maps designed for tracking and flick shots. Then, I play around five to ten matches in Arena Mode to simulate the competitive environment. I try to analyze each match for what I did right and wrong.

Q: What's the biggest challenge you face as a competitive player?
A: Definitely the mental side. You can have all the skills in the world, but if you get tilted after a loss, it messes up your focus. I've learned to take breaks, do some breathing exercises, and stay calm no matter what.

Q: Any advice for players looking to go competitive?
A: Stick to a routine, watch pros, and don't just play—practice with intention. Figure out what you need to improve and dedicate time to it every day. Most importantly, stay positive and don't let losses get you down.

2. Casual Player Story: Mia "Mystic" Lopez
Age: 21
Playstyle: Explorer, Social Player
Favorite Mode: Party Royale
Favorite Event: Travis Scott Concert

Interview:

Q: What do you enjoy most about Fortnite?
A: I love the social side of it! Fortnite isn't just about competition

for me—it's a place to meet up with friends, explore new updates, and just have fun. I'm a huge fan of Party Royale, where we can goof around without worrying about getting eliminated.

Q: What was your favorite Fortnite event?
A: Definitely the Travis Scott concert! The visuals, the music—it was unreal. It felt like a mini-festival, and I got to share it with friends who were halfway across the world. Fortnite does a great job of making virtual events feel like real experiences.

Q: Any tips for casual players?
A: Explore everything Fortnite offers! Try Creative Mode, join events, and don't stress too much about winning. It's more fun when you play for the experience.

3. Creative Mode Designer: Daniel "MapMaster" Chen
Age: 15
Specialty: Custom Map Design
Favorite Build: Obstacle Course Challenge Map

Interview:
Q: How did you get into designing maps in Creative Mode?
A: I started exploring Creative Mode about a year ago, and I was hooked! It's awesome that you can create your own maps and share them with friends. I started by making simple obstacle courses, but now I'm working on escape rooms, puzzle maps, and even small battle arenas.

Q: What's the process like when creating a new map?
A: First, I think of the kind of experience I want players to have. Then, I sketch it out on paper, planning obstacles, checkpoints, and special features. Once I start building, I test each section as I go, making sure it's challenging but not impossible. After it's finished, I'll invite friends to play-test it and give feedback.

Q: Any advice for aspiring Creative Mode designers?
A: Start small and experiment. Learn from other creators by playing their maps and paying attention to the little details. Also, don't be afraid to get feedback and make adjustments.

Profiles of Popular Fortnite Characters

1. Character Spotlight on Jonesy

Backstory: Jonesy is one of Fortnite's most iconic characters, known for his many variants and appearances across multiple seasons. Originally a simple character model, Jonesy has evolved into a central figure within Fortnite's lore, representing the everyman trapped in the Loop, trying to survive and understand the strange forces at play on the island.

Role in the Fortnite Story: Over the seasons, Jonesy has taken on various roles—from a soldier and a survivalist to an undercover agent. His character arc became more complex when he started working with the Imagined Order (IO), a mysterious organization controlling the island's Loop. However, as he learned more about the IO's plans, he joined The Seven, a group determined to free the island from the Loop's endless cycles.

Notable Appearances:

- **Agent Jones**: In Chapter 2, Jonesy became Agent Jones, tasked with managing reality rifts and maintaining the Loop. However, his growing doubts about the IO's intentions led him to rebel.
- **Bunker Jonesy**: A more rugged version of Jonesy who appears as a survivalist, Bunker Jonesy reflects the character's resilience and adaptability in tough situations.

Trivia: Jonesy's character represents the player's journey through Fortnite, adapting to new challenges and constantly evolving. His arc symbolizes the struggle between control and freedom, a central theme in Fortnite's lore.

2. Midas and The Agency

Backstory: Midas is a charismatic and cunning character who led *The Agency*, a secretive organization that wielded significant influence on the island. Known for his golden touch (which literally turned everything he touched into gold), Midas's influence changed the course of Fortnite's story. He introduced The Agency's operatives, each with their own powerful abilities and hidden agendas.

Role in the Fortnite Story: Midas orchestrated "The Device" event, an attempt to break the Loop and control the island's storm. However, his plan backfired, causing massive flooding and chaos. Despite the failure, Midas remains one of the most enigmatic figures, with many fans speculating about his intentions and ultimate goals.

Key Events:

- **The Device Event**: Midas activated a device to disrupt the storm, hoping to control the island's fate. This event led to massive flooding and reshaped the island's landscape.
- **Return and Rumors**: Midas's fate after The Device event is unclear, but references to him appear in subsequent seasons, suggesting he may still be influencing events from behind the scenes.

Trivia: Midas is inspired by the Greek myth of King Midas, who could turn anything he touched into gold. In Fortnite, this power is both his strength and his downfall, as it reflects his desire for control and the unintended consequences of his ambition.

11.6 Tips for Content Creation and Streaming

Getting Started with Streaming

- **Essential Equipment and Setup**: Basics on setting up a stream, including microphone, webcam, and streaming software recommendations.
- **Creating Engaging Content**: Tips on connecting with an audience, maintaining energy, and interacting with viewers through Q&A sessions or shoutouts.
- **Building a Schedule**: The importance of consistency and setting a streaming schedule that aligns with your audience.

Building an Audience

- **Using Social Media**: How to share content on platforms like Twitter, TikTok, and Instagram to grow a following.
- **Collaborating with Other Streamers**: Advice on networking within the Fortnite community, joining collaborative streams, and supporting fellow creators.
- **Engaging with Fans**: Tips on connecting with fans, hosting viewer matches, and creating content that resonates with your audience.

11.7 Personal Journal and Goal-Setting Pages

Goal-Setting Worksheets

- **SMART Goals Template**: A template for setting specific, measurable, achievable, relevant, and time-bound (SMART) goals in Fortnite.
- **Monthly Goal Tracker**: A page where players can set monthly objectives, track progress, and note achievements.
- **Weekly Reflection Pages**: Prompts for players to reflect on what they practiced, learned, and want to improve in the following week.

Progress Tracking Pages

- **Daily Practice Log**: A page for players to log their daily practice routines, skills worked on, and specific challenges encountered.
- **Tournament Preparation and Results**: Dedicated pages to prepare for tournaments, with space to outline strategies, note team dynamics, and reflect on match outcomes.
- **Highlight Reel Section**: A section for players to record memorable in-game moments, strategies that worked, and lessons learned from both successes and challenges.

Personal Journal Pages

- **Customizable Journal Entries**: Blank journal pages where players can document their Fortnite journey, write about memorable matches, or sketch out new strategies.
- **Positive Reinforcement Prompts**: Pages that encourage players to focus on achievements, reflect on skill improvement, and maintain a growth mindset.

Practice Log & Goal-Setting

SMART Goals for This Week:
- Specific: What skill do I want to improve?
- Measurable: How will I know I'm progressing?
- Achievable: Is this realistic with my schedule?
- Relevant: How does this help my overall game?
- Time-Bound: By when do I aim to achieve this?

Examples:
- Improve building speed by practicing 90s in Creative Mode for 30 minutes daily.
- Increase accuracy by 10% in target drills by the end of the week.

Date	Skill Focus	Practice Routine	Duration	Notes

Weekly Reflection & Progress Tracking

Reflection Questions:
1. What skill did I focus on improving this week?
2. What went well in my practice sessions?
3. What challenges did I face, and how can I overcome them?
4. Did I meet my goals? If not, what can I adjust?

Next Steps:
List specific goals for the next week based on this reflection.

Skill	Start of Week Level	End of Week Level	Improvement (%)	Notes

Daily Journal & Highlight Reel

Today's Highlights:

Match Highlights:
- Note any memorable moments or key wins.
- Describe any major strategies that worked well.

New Skills or Tactics Learned:

Areas for Improvement:

Reflection:
- What went well today?
- What can I focus on tomorrow to improve?

THANK YOU PAGE

Thank you for choosing Fortnite Ultimate Strategies and Secrets! I hope this book inspires you to dive deeper into Fortnite and explore new possibilities on the island. Whether you're a casual player, competitive enthusiast, or creative builder, this guide is for you. Remember, every game is a new opportunity to learn, grow, and have fun. Keep pushing your limits, experimenting with new strategies, and connecting with the amazing Fortnite community. I can't wait to see how you use the skills and tips in this book to make your mark in Fortnite. Good luck, and happy gaming!

Made in the USA
Columbia, SC
08 December 2024